THINGS YOU SHOULD KNOW BEFORE ADOPTING

THE PRO'S, THE CON'S, AND ALL THE REST

SAMANTHA EVANS

CONTENTS

Things You Should Know Before Adopting — v

1. Adoption in the Course of History — 1
2. Decision-Making in Adoption — 6
3. Handling the Process of Adoption — 9
4. Adapting to Adoptive Parenting — 12
5. Establishing the Connection — 14
6. Adoption: Looking at Both Sides of the Coin — 17
7. Pros and Cons of Open Adoption for the Adopted Person — 18
8. Pros and Cons of Open Adoption for the Birth Parents — 21
9. Pros and Cons of Open Adoption for the Adoptive Parents — 23
10. Transracial Adoption: Pros and Cons — 25

Section 2: Things Your Adopted Child Will Want To Know About Adoption — 29

Introduction — 31

11. Why Tell Your Child the Truth — 32
12. Prepare Yourself — 34
13. The Process of Telling — 38
14. Explaining Adoption — 40
15. Reason He Was Given Up for Adoption — 47
16. How to Address Your Child's Feelings — 48

THINGS YOU SHOULD KNOW BEFORE ADOPTING

The Pro's, The Con's, And All The Rest

Samantha Evans

1

ADOPTION IN THE COURSE OF HISTORY

Adopted children, during the 1600s and 1700s, were almost exclusively placed to live with relatives. Such time, adopted children served as apprentices for the adoptive family. In the 1800s adoption was mainly pursued because the family needs a helper at home or in their farms. Homeless children that were adopted during such times, however, were not considered equal with biological children. During 1920s, adoption of non-related children began in some parts of the United States. Nine years after, 20 states' statutes legitimized this kind of adoption, better known as, stranger adoption. Between 1920s and 1930s, permanent adoption received social workers' skepticism. They were said to be reluctant with the process of permanent adoption mainly because they were uncertain of the client's ability to genuinely love non-birth children.

During this time, social workers also believed that children must not be given to adoptive parents after birth for children must undergo some observation for the first few months to identify flaws in character, health and intellect.

Only when the child is observed to be healthy in all aspects, can he be viewed by social workers to be suitable for adoption. It was only after the World War II that social workers started supporting permanent placement adoption. Nonetheless, they believe that adoption must be professionally supervised.

Between 1937 and 1945, cases of adoption tripled and from 1945 to 1957 the number of the cases doubled. The Child Welfare League in 1948 averred that every child, without exemption, is fit for adoption. In 1957, the view of social workers regarding adoption as early as child birth changed. The disagreement displayed before turned into the notion that for a child to experience the usual situation of childbirth, it is best for adoptive families to take them home as early as possible.

The process of adoption in the past includes a social worker looking for women with appropriate dress, hairstyle and other characteristics of femininity. From the pool of prospective mothers, the ones showing domestic skills will be the ones chosen. Moreover, if a woman would like to adopt, she must be unemployed. In addition, she must also be able to present some evidence that she and her husband are unable to have their own biological child.

From late 1930's to 1970's, birth records were sealed. Closed adoption was implemented during these times to protect all the parties involved in the process. With closed adoption, birth parents can be protected from the stigma attached to pregnancy outside marriage; adoptive parents can be protected as well from the stigma of inability to procreate; and the adopted child can be protected from the stigma of being born out of wedlock. Closed type of adoption was therefore born in a society where substantial public stigma is associated with adoption itself.

During the said time, adoption agencies strongly believed that it is best for birth mothers to pretend that they never really had a child and for adoptive parents to pretend that the child was theirs' biologically. Moreover, it was thought that the adopted child would feel more whole if he never knew that he was adopted. How adoption is viewed depends largely on the societal standards of a specific time. Sixty years after, societal changes paved way to the consideration of openness in adoption. The idea that there is a need to protect people involved in the adoption process began to diminish.

During the 1980's parties involved in adoption became more open with their experiences that in turn made the public more aware of the numbers of people "hurt" with the secrecy of adoption. The following years starting from 1990s offered more acceptance and preference with open adoption. Lesser stigma has been associated with pregnancy outside marriage, and infertility became a common topic in discussions since larger numbers of people tend to experience it.

Understanding the Concept

WHAT IS ADOPTION?

In the contemporary times, adoption referred to the legal action that terminates rights, privileges, duties and relationships between the child and the birth mother and/or father, and any person acting as the legal parent of the child.

CATEGORIES OF ADOPTION

Adoption can be classified in different ways. Adoption

agencies usually use three main categories of adoption namely private international, private domestic and public domestic. International adoption refers to the transfer of children from one nation to another for parenting purposes. This kind of adoption can be viewed as the extreme case of what is labeled stranger adoption. Domestic adoption refers to adopting children born in the United States, which includes adopting from birth parents, foster parents and foster homes.

Private domestic adoption involves private adoption agencies, whether non-profit or profit oriented organizations. Such agencies offer a wide array of services, which includes finding children, profiling children and birth parents, counseling for birth parents and adoptive parents, temporary foster care for children and legal help. Public adoption typically involves children taken from unfit or abusive parents.

Another classification of adoption usually used by social workers involves two categories: open adoption and closed adoption. This type of classification is based on the kind and frequency of interaction present between the child and his/her birth parents. When the birth mother is in regular contact with the child she has given up for adoption and the adoptive family, it is a kind of an open adoption. Closed adoption on the other hand, happens when the birth parents do not really know who adopted the child and have no contact of any kind with them and the child.

Another classification of adoption used by some agencies includes two categories that go by the name "traditional" and "minority." White adoptive parents adopting a white child, or non-white parents adopting a non-white child, will characterize the traditional category of adoption while adoption of white couple to a non-white child or non-white parents adopting a white child will fall in the minority category.

2

DECISION-MAKING IN ADOPTION

There can be varying reasons why a family or a couple would want to resort to adoption to raise a kid. Some families would like to add another member of the family and choose adoption to fulfill the need. Some couples just happened to be unable to produce their own offspring while others just wanted to help abandoned children. These are just some of the possible situations that would push people to consider adoption.

Whatever the reason behind adoption, one must not forget that this is a major decision that must be thought of rigorously. There are several factors that must be considered before deciding on the matter. Adoption will bring major change in the family's life; thus, deciding as a family will be necessary. There must be a significant and objective self-reflection for the adoptive parents before pursuing the process. The reasons why they want to adopt must be crystal clear to them.

The following are questions taken from *Child Welfare Information Gateway,* Children's Bureau/Administration on Children, Youth and Family that will be of great help for couples and families planning to pursue adoption.

- How will a new child fit into the parents' lives and their relationship?
- How will a new child affect family dynamics—especially if the family already has children?
- What changes are the parents willing to make to ease the child's transition?
- How do the parents feel about "open" adoption, that is, contact with the child's birth family?
- How do the parents feel about welcoming a child from the foster care system or an orphanage who may have experienced abuse or neglect?
- In cases of transracial or transcultural adoption—how do the parents feel about accommodating, helping, and promoting the child's positive cultural and racial identity?
- How will the parents inform family members and friends, and how they will deal with questions from family, friends, and strangers about adoption?
- How will the parents answer their child's questions about adoption, the child's background and history, birth family, and the parents' reasons for adoption?
- How willing and able are they to seek help for themselves or their child when necessary?

By answering the questions provided above, one will be able to objectively guide the family's decision-making process regarding the plan of adoption. Indeed, there are several factors that must be looked at and explored to see things in a bigger picture. Adoption is a serious matter that must be dealt with accordingly. One cannot just change his mind along the process for there are several parties and feelings involved.

3

HANDLING THE PROCESS OF ADOPTION

After going through the decision-making phase, another stage that couples and families must go through is the process of adoption itself. Unfortunately for prospective parents, the process of adoption is not just about signing papers and all. The process is more of an overly burdensome and intrusive kind of experience for some.

The laws accompanying the adoption process vary across states. Depending on the type of adoption a couple is aiming at, additional laws might be applicable.

Among the very first thing the couple must decide on in the process of adoption is the kind of adoption they will make. Are they going to consider inter-country or domestic adoption? Will they ask help from an adoption agency? If yes, which one and how to choose? How are they going to deal with home study questions? These are just some of the initial concerns that prospective parents must be able to address.

Also the process of adoption takes time thus; couples must be able to pack a bag of patience while going through the process. There are also planned factors and details that can delineate from the original plan of adoption. It is possible for a placement of the specific child chosen or preferred, to happen anytime. Moreover, since the process will take some time, there are several opportunities for uncertain outcomes to happen. There are several possibilities, for instance, the birth parents suddenly changed their minds regarding adoption or a relative suddenly decided to take custody of the child instead. Such events can happen and could hinder a couple's plan of adopting a child.

Prospective parents must also be prepared to submit requirements that usually involve the following; proof of income with tax return, proof of health with medical records, proof of qualification with recommendation letters and proof of marriage with a copy of marriage certificate. Different adoption agencies require varying documentations and other qualifications necessary for the adoption. Some would require a proof that at least one of the couple would take time off from employment after receiving the child. Others would even require that adoptive parents have no biological child. For couple with biological children, some agencies would have a maximum and minimum age range for their children as a requirement for eligibility for adoption.

The cost of adoption is another matter that must be known for prospective parents prior the adoption process. Public adoption is most probably the most affordable type, costing at least $2000; nonetheless, more often than not, children available through public agencies are usually teenagers and children with serious disabilities. This group is commonly referred to as "hard-to-place" children. Private adoptions usually cost between $10,000 and $12,000. The most expensive type of adoption is the international one. To complete this adoption process, one needs $20,000 to $35,000.

After the prospective parents have completed the requirements for the adoption, they will still wait for months or even a year before they receive the child. The waiting time differs for it largely depends on the availability of children. Parents usually request for children with specific characteristics during the process. The characteristics specified will make the waiting time longer. For instance, a couple requested for a white child; the waiting period will take as long as 18 months. A request for a black child, however, will just take one to nine months. This trend is primarily because there are more black kids available for adoption than white ones.

4

ADAPTING TO ADOPTIVE PARENTING

Studies show that majority of the adoptive parents are satisfied with their decision. Nevertheless, some difficulties can still be experienced in the post adoption period.

Post Adoption Depression Syndrome or PADS is the feeling of sadness or being "let down" after months of anticipating parenthood. This, according to researches, usually occurs within a few weeks of the completion of adoption. Becoming a parent is not as easy as how one imagines it. The weight of the responsibilities associated with becoming actual parents can be overwhelming for some, especially for first-time parents. Creating an attachment with the child might not be easy and sometimes several efforts fail, making the parent feel incapable of becoming an effective guardian for the child.

For couples who adopt infants, it must be expected that there will be some sleepless nights, a lot of diaper changing and other tiresome tasks that must be accomplished accordingly and in a timely manner. Most of the time, these parenting realities make a parent question his/her capability of becoming a parent for a child. There are going to be moments when parents would feel insufficient to deserve becoming a mother or a father to the adopted child.

Fortunately, parents tend to overcome the depression, as they adjust to the new life. Nonetheless, if the depression persisted for several weeks and is interfering with the productivity and functioning of the parent involved, a professional help must be sought.

Once a family decided on adopting a child, they are as well deciding on major changes in their life. Everyone's role will have significant changes once the child arrives home with his/her new parents. Most of the time, such changes in the role, no matter how subtle it is, can make a person feel different in one way or another. The couple is now a mother and a father. The adopted child is now part of a new family. If the couple has a biological son/daughter, then his/her role will change into a brother or a sister. Adjusting to the new roles is the part that is never easy. The arrival of the adopted child would seem to push through drastic changes in the family.

Attachments and love are the common emotional grounds that seem to be difficult to establish in the new family setting. Some adopted children will have the feeling of alienation within the new family system. For the parents, connecting with the child and making him/her feel "at home" can be challenging. Some parents can easily be disheartened by seeing their efforts to create a bond produce too little or no effect at all. Some parents are troubled with how to start establishing connections with the child.

5

ESTABLISHING THE CONNECTION

What bothers most adoptive parents is the feeling that no sort of bond or connection seems to flow naturally even if the adopted child is living with the family already. The problem sometimes is that parents want result too quickly. They must realize that the child needs time to adjust with the major changes in his/her life. Moreover, how long would the adjustment period is cannot be foretold for it will largely depend on the child's way of coping and adjusting. Therefore, parents must give the child the time he/she needs, but at the same time they must not halt efforts in trying to show love and affection, after all the kid is theirs now.

If connection does not come in naturally, then establish it. One way for parents to help the process of building a relationship with the adopted child is through engaging the child in all family activities. Creating a family ritual would be of great help. The child must feel involved with everything the family is concerned of, so he/she will gradually be removed from the prison of alienation.

Making the child feel important is also pivotal. An

adopted child might have bad experiences with her biological family; thus letting her know and feel that her new family is a lot different in a good way might encourage her to meet the parents' efforts half-way with her own.

Creating a family photo book would also help the child feel included in the family. Once a child sees that her photos are included in the family book, then she will have the feeling of belongingness. Take pictures of the whole family and put them in frames to be displayed around the house. This will also help the child adjust in his/her new family setting easier.

Another way is the very basic technique of getting to know the child personally. Primarily, the adoption agency must have given valuable information about the child and his/her background. Nonetheless, knowing the child personally will make parents more connected to the child, and vice versa. Establishing a relationship always starts from the getting-to-know stage; parents must do this to achieve the desired kind of relationship with the adopted kid. Parents must find time to converse with the kid. At first, this might not be easy for the parents might receive silence for answers. Nonetheless, this is not a reason to give up; it is actually a reason to continue. An unfaltering effort pays.

Knowing another couple that adopted a child 2 to 10 years ago will be helpful in the process. Sharing experiences with them might give encouragements and new perspectives to new parents. Learning from their stories of adjustments will give parents new strategies to try. Nonetheless, parents must keep in mind that everyone is unique and so are situations. Hence, one must not expect that every strategy or technique that worked for one family will work for his/her own.

Lastly, parents must be prepared with answers. The

child will definitely ask things he/she cannot understand. By that time, one must be able to have satisfying answers. In addition to this, other people will definitely ask several questions; thus, one must have answers readily available.

If parents think that the child's adjustment is taking so long or their own adjustment is, then they must help the adjustment process itself. Adjustment is a process; parents must give it the time necessary while nourishing areas like love, affection and care that are pivotal to the establishment of a strong bond and relationship with the adopted child.

6

ADOPTION: LOOKING AT BOTH SIDES OF THE COIN

There are several issues concerning adoption and among the most controversial includes open adoption and transracial adoption. Whether these kinds of adoption are proper or improper, helpful or destructive is still debated until now. This part of the book will present both sides of the coin starting with open adoption.

Open adoption, as discussed earlier, is a kind of adoption whereby adoptive parents and birth parents share information and contacts before, during and even after the process of adoption has been completed.

7

PROS AND CONS OF OPEN ADOPTION FOR THE ADOPTED PERSON

The benefits of open adoption involve the creation of an enhanced sense of self by the adopted person. With the traditional closed adoption, the agency will not disclose any information about the child's biological parents. Thus, nothing can be known about the child's biological origins. The reason why open adoption is supported by most experts in this area is because of the alarming cases of heightened identity confusion displayed by adopted children. With open adoption, the child will be fully knowledgeable of his/her full heritage.

Open adoption will allow the person adopted to know his/her self holistically. Accurate information about the adopted person's cultural and ethnic background will be gained from open adoption. Moreover, accurate medical data can be possessed. This is very important to fully assess the adopted person, medically speaking. In case he/she develops certain illness in life, a complete and precise medical history will be of great help in finding appropriate treatment and/or medication.

The adopted person will also be freed from any emotional impact caused by knowing nothing about his own origin. It is very common for an adopted person to feel "incomplete" once he has learned about his adoption. Regardless if the adoptive parents were able to provide sufficient love, care and affection to the adopted son, he will still suffer some emotional trouble because of the belief that the majority of who he is remains unknown.

Open adoption will also eliminate any misconceptions the adopted person might develop due to the secrecy of the identity of his/her real parents. It is also more likely that the person adopted will take the situation in a more mature manner. Open adoption eliminates haunting questions; thus, saving the individual from the trouble of running away.

Indeed there are significant advantages of open adoption for the person adopted. Nonetheless, there are also drawbacks with this kind of openness.

With open adoption, the adoptee can access the information of his/her biological parents and can pursue meeting them. Also, the person can opt not to see or know them personally. When the former is chosen by the child, it cannot be avoided for the adoptive parents to be hurt. If the adoptee wants to avoid hurting them, but is emotionally troubled by the feeling of incompleteness, then he should know that open adoption can cause more emotional uncertainty than closed adoption. Sometimes knowing more brings complication rather than solution.

Another drawback of open adoption is the notion that the child is unwanted by his/her biological parents. It is an inevitable thought especially for the adopted person. This idea can trigger hatred to biological parents and even to oneself. For a person to know that he was given away by his own parents will definitely stir negative concepts about oneself.

8

PROS AND CONS OF OPEN ADOPTION FOR THE BIRTH PARENTS

Open Adoption can offer several benefits for the biological parents, as well. Perhaps, nothing is more important for a birth parent than to know that his/her child is in good hands. With open adoption, birth parents will know the kind of family who will raise his/her child. This will ease the anxiety and fear that the birth parents are experiencing. In addition, the grieving process will not be very difficult for the biological parents if they are well-informed of the child's where-about.

Open adoption will also open opportunities for the birth parents to discuss the matter of adoption with the child. With closed adoption, there is no way for the biological parents to explain to the adopted person why he/she was given up for adoption.

The biological parents will also have the chance to still be involved with the child's life. Provided that this kind of setting is agreed upon by the adoptive parents, birth parents need not be strangers for the adopted person.

Open adoption, however, can also post disadvantages for the biological parents. Emotions are just so strong at times that even if birth parents were able to provide the reason for adoption together with other answers to the adopted person's questions; the adoptee will still resent him. Hatred directly addressed to a birth mother/father will be very painful.

With open adoption, other people not directly involved with the adoption matter can place judgments upon the birth parents. In a conservative social context, neighbors might attach stigma to the birth parents for sending their child for adoption. A stigma is never an easy matter that a person can be over with after a short while. Negative notions about them placed by the judging eyes of the neighborhood will definitely cause emotional troubles for the biological parents. This is exactly what closed adoption is avoiding. Secrecy somehow can protect birth parents from unwanted judgments and unsolicited opinion coming from other people, who, most probably, have the least understanding of the situation.

9

PROS AND CONS OF OPEN ADOPTION FOR THE ADOPTIVE PARENTS

Some of the advantages of open adoption for the adoptive parents include the ability to be involved in pre-birth doctor's visits until delivery. This allows adoptive parents to be assured that the birth mother is in good and healthy condition during pregnancy. If they can assist the biological mother with the pregnancy and later on delivery of the child, then a strong feeling of connection with the child prior to his birth will be established by the adoptive parents. With this, building connections with the non-biological child later on will not be that difficult.

The openness of information in adoption will also allow adoptive parents to eliminate the fear of the unknown. This, perhaps, is the most promising advantage of open adoption. Among the fears that adoptive parents might have include the possibility that one day, the child's biological parents will come knocking on their door to get the him/her.

The disadvantages of open adoption for the adoptive parents may include the fear and possibility that the adopted child will choose his/her biological parents over them. Adoptive parents will always have such concern; that despite their efforts to become the best parents they could possibly be for the child, blood might be really thicker than water.

Role confusion can also be stirred by open adoption. Having a child with two mothers and two fathers is a confusing family set-up. The ambiguity of where a parent's (biological and non-biological) responsibility starts and ends can serve as a hindrance in making this complicated family system work.

These are just some of the pros and cons of adopting a child through an open adoption. The lives of all the parties involved in such kind of adoption might be more complicated in actual everyday experiences than how they appear in texts. Adopting a child is indeed a major decision with positive and negative impact that must be dealt with for a very long period of time, perhaps even a lifetime.

10

TRANSRACIAL ADOPTION: PROS AND CONS

Another major concern in the adoption arena involves transracial adoption. This refers to a couple adopting a child who belongs to a different cultural heritage. Whether this kind of adoption is helpful or mainly disruptive is a major debate that runs until now.

THE CONS

One major claim that opponents of transracial adoption state is that a white family adopting a black child can harm the child in the process. According to opponents, only parents belonging to the same racial origin can offer an effective parenting to the child. For instance, only black parents can teach a black child the proper way of dealing with racism. This is primarily because they, as blacks, most probably have experienced dealing with such. According to opponents, a white family cannot address this important aspect effectively mainly because they lack any experience related to the issue of racism. As stated by critics of transracial adoption, for a child to meet an appropriate psychological development, he/she must be placed with parents of the same cultural orientation.

Another claim is that adoptive parents are also harmed in the process of transracial adoption. White parents will likely be subjected to intrusiveness, hostility and/or prejudice for adopting transracially. For instance, people surrounding a white couple will not easily get used to the fact that they adopted a black kid. Interviews conducted to white parents reveal that they receive intrusive questions from immediate family and friends just because of transracial adoption. The physical difference alone would make other people wonder about the situation. In addition to this, parents who adopted transracially usually receive "the look" or "the stare" from other people that is very much unpleasant.

On the other hand, supporters of transracial adoption maintain that this kind of adoption offers unique benefits for the children. A permanent and healthy home is what a child needs. Racial matching must not be the priority especially if it can cause delay to the opportunity for a child to have a family.

The relationship between the adoptive parents and the child is also deemed deeper and stronger primarily because the bond was not forced by biological-relatedness rather it was built entirely from the foundation of the bond itself.

The obvious physical differences will also serve as reminders for parents that the child is adopted. The good thing about this is that parents will have more reasons to accept the child as he/she is; thus, avoiding setting unreasonable expectations of likeness in abilities and personalities brought by false biological relationship.

In addition to this, people who adopt transracially display an admirable trait which makes them the most qualified individuals to adopt. If a couple does not look at race as an important aspect in adoption, then they see no difference among children belonging to different cultural heritages. They are parents who are usually well educated about treating everyone equally. Moreover, parents who opt to adopt transracially are showing high-levels of commitment in the process of adoption.

Among the "stranger" adoption types, transracial adoption posts the most challenge. Parents involve in such adoption must have to deal with cultural differences aside from biological un-relatedness. By adopting a child from different race, parents show more commitment for despite the awareness that this kind of adoption is the most challenging of all, they still pursue the process.

Transracial adoption can also benefit the society itself. Having families, composed of parents and children from different cultural heritage, around will reduce societal racism and racial tension. Witnessing that people from different race can become one and united as a family will make people realize that the color of the skin is not an important aspect of the human life.

Parents who adopt transracially can also offer a new perspective to the society whose conception of a family and race remains traditional. Parents who adopted children from different race are racially open-minded even before receiving the child. Moreover, these parents revealed through interviews that they became more accepting to others after adopting transracially.

Prejudice is most likely attributed to the lack of social contact. People feel different from one another because there is no ground that would let them know each other in a deeper manner. Having families with adopted children from different cultural heritage can be a good start to eliminate prejudice and racism in the entire society.

SECTION 2: THINGS YOUR ADOPTED CHILD WILL WANT TO KNOW ABOUT ADOPTION

Things Your Adopted Child Will Want To Know About Adoption

INTRODUCTION

Every parent of an adopted child wonders when, how, and if they should tell the child about adoption. This book offers strategies and techniques, and ways to inform the child about his or her adoption; and reasons to explain why you wanted to adopt.

This book goes into detail and explains the questions that are going through your child's mind, relating to birth parents, and being equally loved to your birth children.

It also explains how to expect the child to feel after he or she has been told she is adopted as well as strategies to keep the child feeling loved. These are only a few of the many topics that will be touched on in this book. For simplicity purposes, I am going to refer to the child as "him" or "he" throughout the book.

11

WHY TELL YOUR CHILD THE TRUTH

Normally for children raised by their biological parents, facts about themselves are not kept and are something known ever since they can handle comprehension. But for children who are raised and cared for by adoptive parents, knowing who they really are is a necessity and a potentially life-changing event. For the parents who cared and loved these children even if they are not biologically related, letting the story of adoption slip from their mouth is something that can be dreadful, tough, and painful. Some, due to fear of what may happen, would even decide they would never tell their children they are adopted. But that will only occur in a parent's mind if she does not know what to do, when to do it, and how to prepare her child about these things.

Keeping your child's adoption story from him is basically stealing a part of his identity. It will only lead to something irreparable—it would break down your relationship with him. You cannot stop him from wondering why he seems different—especially when he gets older. And worse, there is a great chance he will learn from someone else that he is adopted. He would feel betrayed and speculate about the reasons he was left by his biological parents. It would be so much harder for both of you.

Furthermore, for adopted transracial children, the increase in their interest about their being different is something unavoidable. Hence, it would be wise to start the process of telling the story of his adoption once he reaches the age when he can already comprehend things.

Every child deserves to know who they truly are. Having full knowledge about oneself greatly increases self-esteem and self-worth. Everyone simply needs to learn their past in order for them to look forward to and build their future.

12

PREPARE YOURSELF

Before we go down to the flow of the process, it is essential for you to be ready. The shock and pain you may feel can be equal to what your child may experience when he is told about his adoption. Though you can only guess what would happen when your child finally know that he is adopted—whether it will turn out to be easy for both of you or not—if you prepare yourself for the worst, hope for the best, and accept whatever the outcome will be, things will be easier for you.

BELOW IS a strategy that can help you ready yourself. Every step here contains "**what to expect**" and "**what to hope**" parts as well as explanation to back it up.

WHAT TO EXPECT

Expect your child to be shocked and depressed when he finally hears that he is adopted.

. . .

WHAT TO HOPE

Hope that after whatever he felt, or however shocked he is, he will still calmly and peacefully accept that he is adopted.

Your child can hardly handle distressing situations like this. Give him time and space to comprehend things properly and let him think things over.

WHAT TO EXPECT

Expect that he will be mad at you because of keeping the story of adoption from him.

WHAT TO HOPE

Hope that over time, he will recognize that you do not need to be his birth parent for the two of you to have a real parent-child relationship.

Your child may feel betrayed because you kept the truth from him for a time. This is natural. But after a while, he will work out that he is loved and there is no reason for him to be livid at you.

WHAT TO EXPECT

Expect him to feel he is worthless, abandoned, and incomplete.

WHAT TO HOPE

Hope that he will soon see that it is not because of him

but because of his birth parents that he was given up for adoption.

It is natural for a child to feel that the reason he was given away is because there's something wrong with him. But because of the unparalleled love you have shown and are showing him, he will realize how perfect he is in your eyes.

WHAT TO EXPECT

Your relationship with him will never be as good as it was before you told him about the adoption.

WHAT TO HOPE

Hope that as time passes, your child will realize how much you love him.

Upon knowing he's adopted, he may feel a little conscious being with you because he may still have the desire to know who his birth parents are and why they gave him up for adoption. But that desire—achieved or not—will not stop your child from longing for your love.

WHAT TO EXPECT

Your child will start to think that you love your birth children more than him.

WHAT TO HOPE

Hope that with the effort you exert to keep your relationship with him at par with what you have with your biological kids, he will realize that you love all your children – including him - equally.

It is natural for him to think of that. Hence, it is important that you never skimp on the love and attention you give your child. Nothing should change. Show him that he is your child no matter what.

13

THE PROCESS OF TELLING

Telling your child about the adoption is a lifelong process. Time is an important factor here. It is crucial that you plan about this even before adopting, and set it in motion while he is still young. It does not necessarily mean you should tell him right away that he is adopted. But there are small steps that you can take. Every step should be according to his intellectual and emotional maturity level. The process starts with shaping his view of adoption. If a child does not have a positive view on it, it will be harder for him to accept the fact that he is adopted.

AGES 1-5

Children within this age bracket think the world revolves around them. They think literally and one-dimensionally. Their brains start to burst with questions regarding things that seem alien to them—including adoption and pregnancy. So it is highly important to know how to react properly on their queries.

Your child's curiosity is your signal for you to start the

explanation. But if you don't see it coming, you can go ahead and discuss the said topics with him.

EXPLAINING *Pregnancy to Your Child*

In order for your child to identify adoption from pregnancy, tell him the purpose of pregnancy from a juvenile perspective. It is also very important to focus on the birth process and make sure to involve your child in your explanation.

Here's a sample explanation:

"Harry, pregnancy is the process of keeping a baby inside his mommy's tummy because his parents love him and they want him to live in this world with them. Mothers give birth to their children because having a child is the best feeling a parent can have."

14

EXPLAINING ADOPTION

In order for him to have a good understanding of adoption, explain it too in a way he can understand.

For example, your story can go like this:

"Harry, adoption happens because someone really wants to have and love a child."

EXPLAINING **That Adoption is Equal to the Birth Process**

For him to fully grasp adoption as an entirely good thing, explain that adoption and the birth process are similar.

Your story should go like this:

"Harry, it is not important how parents have their child. What is important is that they love him. Adoption and giving birth are both good ways of having a child. Some kids are lucky they were both born and adopted."

EXPLAINING **Why He or She is Different**

If your child is different in race, or entirely distinct in physical features, he will easily become aware of his being different from you. But at this age bracket, he needs assurance that he is your child and you should prevent him from feeling he is an outcast. It doesn't necessarily mean you should disclose the facts about his birth parents right away. Explain it to him in a manner that he can understand and accept.

If your child asks why he's different, you can phrase your answer this way:

"Harry, we might be a little different in terms of the color of our skin or eyes or hair, but remember that we love you. People are different from one another. It's just like how books need different titles so we don't get confused. See, no one is identical. And your uniqueness will not stop me from loving you."

In order for your child to have a positive view of adoption, it might be wise to tell him or her bedtime stories that include adopted characters. Or watch movies with him that include characters who are adopted. Choose the ones that will help him grasp adoption whole-heartedly.

Also, remember that this is not a one-shot process. The tips above should be done consistently and whenever necessary.

FOR A CHILD **between the Ages 6 and 9**

Your child, within this age period, already has a broader understanding of the different ways of having a child. He already has a clear perspective on adoption. And most importantly, you and your child probably have already established a close and warm relationship. This is the time that he is closest to you; hence, telling him about his adoption at this stage can minimize the emotional impact this news may have on him.

When telling his adoption story, avoid being matter-of-faculty if the facts regarding his parents are something his innocence cannot yet take or something that can make him upset about his parents as well as himself. For example, you wouldn't tell to your child his mother gave birth to him when she was 17, or that her mother was an alcoholic. What you should tell him instead is that his birth parents love him and they want him to have a better future that's why he was put up for adoption.

After telling your child, he will start to feel abandoned or neglected. He will start to speculate about the reasons he was "given away". Children handle this depressing time in their own way. Some openly talk about it; some are reclusive and fake their feelings; some are agitated about it; and some don't care about their adoption story. The best you can do is to offer your shoulder to him. Ask your child how he feels and try to understand it.

FOR A CHILD *Between the Ages 9 and 11*

Keeping your child's positive view about adoption does not stop at any age period. Though you are done with explaining the difference of pregnancy and the birth process from adoption, talking about the circumstances surrounding his birth is crucial. At this age period, your child will sporadically experience extreme feelings of loss, grief, incompleteness, and a yearning for his birth parents – their identity as well as their present whereabouts.

Some of the questions that may be nagging your child are the following:

- Do my birth parents love me?
- If they love me, why did they leave me?
- So many single-parents live happily with their child, why was my mother not able to do the same with me?
- Couldn't my parents have sacrificed for me?
- Where are they now?
- How are they now?
- Do my adoptive parents love me?

YOUR CHILD MAY FEEL a little hatred towards his birth parents because it is still hard for him to accept the fact that he is adopted. At the same time, he might also doubt the love you are showing him. What you need to do is to keep an ongoing and open dialogue with him. Remember that this ordeal is a challenge both the adoptive parents and the child should face.

Regarding how those questions should be answered, at this age period, uncovering facts that may still make him feel upset about his fate and that of his parents is not yet appropriate. Telling life's various gloomy circumstances is still beyond his understanding and emotional coverage. What you should do instead is to defend his birth parents. Diminish the hatred he is feeling towards his birth parents by assuring him that they love him, and then turn the spotlight on you two. For example, when answering the question:

"So many single-parents live happily with their child, why was my mother not able to do the same with me?"

Do not provide a response that will give your child a

negative view of his parents. Your answer should be something like this:

"Harry, I know it is hard for you. It is hard for me too. But it is much harder for your birth parents. This is because in order for you to have a better life, they gave up the chance to raise you. Harry, your parents must be so brave to face each day without you by their side."

Letting your child build a positive image of his birth parents right now will make it easier for him to digest the truth when he's older.

FORMING **Your Child's Identity**

Adolescence is that part of a person's life where he tries to form his identity far from the world he knew at home. Discovering his talents, exploring other things, reaching for his dreams... This is a crucial phase for him, and so much more crucial for an adopted child if the information about his birth parents and about himself is lacking. You simply should tell him the truth at this point. Furthermore, as they grow old, adopted children will find it hard to fit in the world they're in; this is especially true for trans racial adopted children. Your child may feel and see that he is different when he's at home, given the fact that his skin color is distinct from everyone in the family. Details about their birth parents and about their adoption story are the key for them to fully understand who they are and why they seem so different. As parents, you wouldn't want your child to suffer under the curse of adoption.

Children who are **12-18** years old already have the ability and maturity to accept how adoption changed their fate. Their intellectual and emotional maturity has already grown by leaps and bounds at these ages. Your child can now comprehend the fact that his mother is an alcoholic, or his mother was pregnant at 17, or died giving birth to him. Furthermore, it will be easier for him to understand that there is a reason you didn't disclose these facts to him before.

As your child enters this challenging part of his life, his demands to know more about himself, about his birth parents, and the circumstances that surrounded his adoption story will be stronger. He will now realize that the story of adoption you have provided earlier to him is inadequate. He will start to crave for more factual, deeper, and detailed answers. Your child will also start to think of different reasons just to fill the void you created. But his curiosity can lead him to confusion. His questions will start to involve not only his birth parents but also himself. *"What was wrong with me? Can't they love me? Didn't they want to have a child?"*

It is your responsibility, as an adoptive parent, to keep your child from thinking he's a mistake and/or a failure, or that he doesn't deserve to be loved.

During this age period, these are the issues that should be discussed with him:

FACTS *About The Birth parents*

As your child blooms into a teen, his yearning for the facts about his birth parents becomes inevitable. And at this time, there is no point to continue to tell your child the adoption story you made up when he was younger. He would want the details and the truth from you. As your teenage child grows older, he'd want to have a much deeper understanding of his birth parents. He'd want to feel complete. Though the facts about your child's birth parents are potentially upsetting or harmful, leaving him fantasizing about the reason they left him can be much more antagonizing. Generally, truth is preferred.

REASON HE WAS ADOPTED

Why did you adopt your child? Was it that he was left at your front door? Or was he handed to you by someone you didn't know? Whatever the facts surrounding his adoption, he deserves to know them. Truth be told, there is no reason for you to keep his adoption story from him. Just like when you told him that he is adopted, it would be hard at first. But over time, he'll learn to accept what happened to him.

THE BIRTH PARENTS' *Condition*

Your child, even if he feels hatred towards his birth parents, won't stop thinking about the present condition of his birth parents. These may be among his questions: How are they now? Is my mother still alive? Do I have siblings? Are they okay?

Provide information about his biological family if you can. Not knowing the facts will push your child to think negative thoughts about his birth parents' present condition. Though the truth about their condition can upset or worry him, thinking something negative that isn't really happening is potentially more damaging. Knowing the facts—even if these are difficult to accept—is a relief for your child.

15

REASON HE WAS GIVEN UP FOR ADOPTION

"Was there anything wrong with me?" "Didn't they love me?" "Was I not worth loving?" Your child may also be entertaining these questions.

It is important for your child to know the reason he was put up for adoption and/or left by his parents. He needs to make sense of the whole story of his adoption.

16

HOW TO ADDRESS YOUR CHILD'S FEELINGS

There's no telling how long the emotional turmoil your child's story of adoption can bring him will last. It highly depends on how you involve yourself and how you address his feelings. Even though it is clear your child has finally accepted that he was adopted, he may still feel doubtful about certain things. He might ask these: *Do my adoptive parents love me like they love their birth children? Do they regret of adopting me? Do I deserve their love?*

IT IS normal for him to feel this way. But leaving your child to lick his wounds just like that will not, in any way, eliminate the questions going on inside his mind. You need to maintain a good relationship with him. This chapter will tell you how to keep your relationship with your child as good as it was.

*TALK **to Your Child About School***
During meal times or when there is a chance, try to ask

him how his school-life is going. It is an assurance that you care about his achievements or failures; that you care about him.

ACKNOWLEDGE **His or Her Achievements**

Your child got an A+. How should you react? Well, this tip should apply to all mother-and-child relationships, including that between you and your adopted child. You should simply recognize all the good things he does—whether these are small or big achievements.

AVOID GETTING INFURIATED **When Your Child Fails**

Getting angry at him because of his failures (big or small) can exacerbate his negative feelings towards himself, you, and his biological parents. Though of course being angry at times is unmanageable, and sometimes needed, pick the times when you should let out your anger. Know when anger is not actually needed. Control it if possible.

BOND **with Your Child**

Your time together should not lessen nor change just because something about your child is unveiled. Continue doing your bonding activities, whether it's watching your favorite TV show together, or visiting your favorite theme park. Besides, this is the perfect time for you to show that your love for him has not changed.

. . .

ATTEND *Your Child's School Activities*

Attending school activities, especially those that require parents to go will make him feel he is important to you. Give him the support he needs with school projects and other campus activities.

ASK *How He or She Feels About Adoption*

This step will apply to your child if he's 6-18 years old. Talking to him about his adoption story can actually ease the pain he keeps inside. Show him that it is okay that he is adopted. You need to assure him that his adoption story doesn't make him different from your other children. Ask your child what he feels about it, and respond in a positive way.

THE MOST ESSENTIAL step in helping your child get through this depressing time is keeping all lines of communication open. You two should exchange thoughts. And you should always understand him.

REMEMBER that all the steps given in this book should not be done out of guilt or because you feel forced to do so. Also, the tips given are actually instinctive to parents of adopted kids who really love and care for their child. Maintaining a good relationship with your child—adopted or not—is not a necessity but a responsibility. You love your child because you love him. There should be no other reason for this.

www.ingramcontent.com/pod-product-compliance
Lightning Source LLC
Chambersburg PA
CBHW052125110526
44592CB00013B/1758